VISITOR LOG BOOK

COMPANY	
ADDRESS	
PHONE	
FAX	
EMAIL	
DATE LOG STARTED	
DATE LOG ENDED	

Visitor Sign In Sheet

DATE	VISITOR'S NAME	REASON FOR VISIT	TIME IN	TIME OUT	SIGN / INITIAL

Visitor Sign In Sheet

DATE	VISITOR'S NAME	REASON FOR VISIT	TIME IN	TIME OUT	SIGN / INITIAL

Visitor Sign In Sheet

DATE	VISITOR'S NAME	REASON FOR VISIT	TIME IN	TIME OUT	SIGN / INITIAL

Visitor Sign In Sheet

DATE	VISITOR'S NAME	REASON FOR VISIT	TIME IN	TIME OUT	SIGN / INITIAL

Visitor Sign In Sheet

DATE	VISITOR'S NAME	REASON FOR VISIT	TIME IN	TIME OUT	SIGN / INITIAL

Visitor Sign In Sheet

DATE	VISITOR'S NAME	REASON FOR VISIT	TIME IN	TIME OUT	SIGN / INITIAL

Visitor Sign In Sheet

DATE	VISITOR'S NAME	REASON FOR VISIT	TIME IN	TIME OUT	SIGN / INITIAL

Visitor Sign In Sheet

DATE	VISITOR'S NAME	REASON FOR VISIT	TIME IN	TIME OUT	SIGN / INITIAL

Visitor Sign In Sheet

DATE	VISITOR'S NAME	REASON FOR VISIT	TIME IN	TIME OUT	SIGN / INITIAL

Visitor Sign In Sheet

DATE	VISITOR'S NAME	REASON FOR VISIT	TIME IN	TIME OUT	SIGN / INITIAL

Visitor Sign In Sheet

DATE	VISITOR'S NAME	REASON FOR VISIT	TIME IN	TIME OUT	SIGN / INITIAL

Visitor Sign In Sheet

DATE	VISITOR'S NAME	REASON FOR VISIT	TIME IN	TIME OUT	SIGN / INITIAL

Visitor Sign In Sheet

DATE	VISITOR'S NAME	REASON FOR VISIT	TIME IN	TIME OUT	SIGN / INITIAL

Visitor Sign In Sheet

DATE	VISITOR'S NAME	REASON FOR VISIT	TIME IN	TIME OUT	SIGN / INITIAL

Visitor Sign In Sheet

DATE	VISITOR'S NAME	REASON FOR VISIT	TIME IN	TIME OUT	SIGN / INITIAL

Visitor Sign In Sheet

DATE	VISITOR'S NAME	REASON FOR VISIT	TIME IN	TIME OUT	SIGN / INITIAL

Visitor Sign In Sheet

DATE	VISITOR'S NAME	REASON FOR VISIT	TIME IN	TIME OUT	SIGN / INITIAL

Visitor Sign In Sheet

DATE	VISITOR'S NAME	REASON FOR VISIT	TIME IN	TIME OUT	SIGN / INITIAL

Visitor Sign In Sheet

DATE	VISITOR'S NAME	REASON FOR VISIT	TIME IN	TIME OUT	SIGN / INITIAL

Visitor Sign In Sheet

DATE	VISITOR'S NAME	REASON FOR VISIT	TIME IN	TIME OUT	SIGN / INITIAL

Visitor Sign In Sheet

DATE	VISITOR'S NAME	REASON FOR VISIT	TIME IN	TIME OUT	SIGN / INITIAL

Visitor Sign In Sheet

DATE	VISITOR'S NAME	REASON FOR VISIT	TIME IN	TIME OUT	SIGN / INITIAL

Visitor Sign In Sheet

DATE	VISITOR'S NAME	REASON FOR VISIT	TIME IN	TIME OUT	SIGN / INITIAL

Visitor Sign In Sheet

DATE	VISITOR'S NAME	REASON FOR VISIT	TIME IN	TIME OUT	SIGN / INITIAL

Visitor Sign In Sheet

DATE	VISITOR'S NAME	REASON FOR VISIT	TIME IN	TIME OUT	SIGN / INITIAL

Visitor Sign In Sheet

DATE	VISITOR'S NAME	REASON FOR VISIT	TIME IN	TIME OUT	SIGN / INITIAL

Visitor Sign In Sheet

DATE	VISITOR'S NAME	REASON FOR VISIT	TIME IN	TIME OUT	SIGN / INITIAL

Visitor Sign In Sheet

DATE	VISITOR'S NAME	REASON FOR VISIT	TIME IN	TIME OUT	SIGN / INITIAL

Visitor Sign In Sheet

DATE	VISITOR'S NAME	REASON FOR VISIT	TIME IN	TIME OUT	SIGN / INITIAL

Visitor Sign In Sheet

DATE	VISITOR'S NAME	REASON FOR VISIT	TIME IN	TIME OUT	SIGN / INITIAL

Visitor Sign In Sheet

DATE	VISITOR'S NAME	REASON FOR VISIT	TIME IN	TIME OUT	SIGN / INITIAL

Visitor Sign In Sheet

DATE	VISITOR'S NAME	REASON FOR VISIT	TIME IN	TIME OUT	SIGN / INITIAL

Visitor Sign In Sheet

DATE	VISITOR'S NAME	REASON FOR VISIT	TIME IN	TIME OUT	SIGN / INITIAL

Visitor Sign In Sheet

DATE	VISITOR'S NAME	REASON FOR VISIT	TIME IN	TIME OUT	SIGN / INITIAL

Visitor Sign In Sheet

DATE	VISITOR'S NAME	REASON FOR VISIT	TIME IN	TIME OUT	SIGN / INITIAL

Visitor Sign In Sheet

DATE	VISITOR'S NAME	REASON FOR VISIT	TIME IN	TIME OUT	SIGN / INITIAL

Visitor Sign In Sheet

DATE	VISITOR'S NAME	REASON FOR VISIT	TIME IN	TIME OUT	SIGN / INITIAL

Visitor Sign In Sheet

DATE	VISITOR'S NAME	REASON FOR VISIT	TIME IN	TIME OUT	SIGN / INITIAL

Visitor Sign In Sheet

DATE	VISITOR'S NAME	REASON FOR VISIT	TIME IN	TIME OUT	SIGN / INITIAL

Visitor Sign In Sheet

DATE	VISITOR'S NAME	REASON FOR VISIT	TIME IN	TIME OUT	SIGN / INITIAL

Visitor Sign In Sheet

DATE	VISITOR'S NAME	REASON FOR VISIT	TIME IN	TIME OUT	SIGN / INITIAL

Visitor Sign In Sheet

DATE	VISITOR'S NAME	REASON FOR VISIT	TIME IN	TIME OUT	SIGN / INITIAL

Visitor Sign In Sheet

DATE	VISITOR'S NAME	REASON FOR VISIT	TIME IN	TIME OUT	SIGN / INITIAL

Visitor Sign In Sheet

DATE	VISITOR'S NAME	REASON FOR VISIT	TIME IN	TIME OUT	SIGN / INITIAL

Visitor Sign In Sheet

DATE	VISITOR'S NAME	REASON FOR VISIT	TIME IN	TIME OUT	SIGN / INITIAL

Visitor Sign In Sheet

DATE	VISITOR'S NAME	REASON FOR VISIT	TIME IN	TIME OUT	SIGN / INITIAL

Visitor Sign In Sheet

DATE	VISITOR'S NAME	REASON FOR VISIT	TIME IN	TIME OUT	SIGN / INITIAL

Visitor Sign In Sheet

DATE	VISITOR'S NAME	REASON FOR VISIT	TIME IN	TIME OUT	SIGN / INITIAL

Visitor Sign In Sheet

DATE	VISITOR'S NAME	REASON FOR VISIT	TIME IN	TIME OUT	SIGN / INITIAL

Visitor Sign In Sheet

DATE	VISITOR'S NAME	REASON FOR VISIT	TIME IN	TIME OUT	SIGN / INITIAL

Visitor Sign In Sheet

DATE	VISITOR'S NAME	REASON FOR VISIT	TIME IN	TIME OUT	SIGN / INITIAL

Visitor Sign In Sheet

DATE	VISITOR'S NAME	REASON FOR VISIT	TIME IN	TIME OUT	SIGN / INITIAL

Visitor Sign In Sheet

DATE	VISITOR'S NAME	REASON FOR VISIT	TIME IN	TIME OUT	SIGN / INITIAL

Visitor Sign In Sheet

DATE	VISITOR'S NAME	REASON FOR VISIT	TIME IN	TIME OUT	SIGN / INITIAL

Visitor Sign In Sheet

DATE	VISITOR'S NAME	REASON FOR VISIT	TIME IN	TIME OUT	SIGN / INITIAL

Visitor Sign In Sheet

DATE	VISITOR'S NAME	REASON FOR VISIT	TIME IN	TIME OUT	SIGN / INITIAL

Visitor Sign In Sheet

DATE	VISITOR'S NAME	REASON FOR VISIT	TIME IN	TIME OUT	SIGN / INITIAL

Visitor Sign In Sheet

DATE	VISITOR'S NAME	REASON FOR VISIT	TIME IN	TIME OUT	SIGN / INITIAL

Visitor Sign In Sheet

DATE	VISITOR'S NAME	REASON FOR VISIT	TIME IN	TIME OUT	SIGN / INITIAL

Visitor Sign In Sheet

DATE	VISITOR'S NAME	REASON FOR VISIT	TIME IN	TIME OUT	SIGN / INITIAL

Visitor Sign In Sheet

DATE	VISITOR'S NAME	REASON FOR VISIT	TIME IN	TIME OUT	SIGN / INITIAL

Visitor Sign In Sheet

DATE	VISITOR'S NAME	REASON FOR VISIT	TIME IN	TIME OUT	SIGN / INITIAL

Visitor Sign In Sheet

DATE	VISITOR'S NAME	REASON FOR VISIT	TIME IN	TIME OUT	SIGN / INITIAL

Visitor Sign In Sheet

DATE	VISITOR'S NAME	REASON FOR VISIT	TIME IN	TIME OUT	SIGN / INITIAL

Visitor Sign In Sheet

DATE	VISITOR'S NAME	REASON FOR VISIT	TIME IN	TIME OUT	SIGN / INITIAL

Visitor Sign In Sheet

DATE	VISITOR'S NAME	REASON FOR VISIT	TIME IN	TIME OUT	SIGN / INITIAL

Visitor Sign In Sheet

DATE	VISITOR'S NAME	REASON FOR VISIT	TIME IN	TIME OUT	SIGN / INITIAL

Visitor Sign In Sheet

DATE	VISITOR'S NAME	REASON FOR VISIT	TIME IN	TIME OUT	SIGN / INITIAL

Visitor Sign In Sheet

DATE	VISITOR'S NAME	REASON FOR VISIT	TIME IN	TIME OUT	SIGN / INITIAL

Visitor Sign In Sheet

DATE	VISITOR'S NAME	REASON FOR VISIT	TIME IN	TIME OUT	SIGN / INITIAL

Visitor Sign In Sheet

DATE	VISITOR'S NAME	REASON FOR VISIT	TIME IN	TIME OUT	SIGN / INITIAL

Visitor Sign In Sheet

DATE	VISITOR'S NAME	REASON FOR VISIT	TIME IN	TIME OUT	SIGN / INITIAL

Visitor Sign In Sheet

DATE	VISITOR'S NAME	REASON FOR VISIT	TIME IN	TIME OUT	SIGN / INITIAL

Visitor Sign In Sheet

DATE	VISITOR'S NAME	REASON FOR VISIT	TIME IN	TIME OUT	SIGN / INITIAL

Visitor Sign In Sheet

DATE	VISITOR'S NAME	REASON FOR VISIT	TIME IN	TIME OUT	SIGN / INITIAL

Visitor Sign In Sheet

DATE	VISITOR'S NAME	REASON FOR VISIT	TIME IN	TIME OUT	SIGN / INITIAL

Visitor Sign In Sheet

DATE	VISITOR'S NAME	REASON FOR VISIT	TIME IN	TIME OUT	SIGN / INITIAL

Visitor Sign In Sheet

DATE	VISITOR'S NAME	REASON FOR VISIT	TIME IN	TIME OUT	SIGN / INITIAL

Visitor Sign In Sheet

DATE	VISITOR'S NAME	REASON FOR VISIT	TIME IN	TIME OUT	SIGN / INITIAL

Visitor Sign In Sheet

DATE	VISITOR'S NAME	REASON FOR VISIT	TIME IN	TIME OUT	SIGN / INITIAL

Visitor Sign In Sheet

DATE	VISITOR'S NAME	REASON FOR VISIT	TIME IN	TIME OUT	SIGN / INITIAL

Visitor Sign In Sheet

DATE	VISITOR'S NAME	REASON FOR VISIT	TIME IN	TIME OUT	SIGN / INITIAL

Visitor Sign In Sheet

DATE	VISITOR'S NAME	REASON FOR VISIT	TIME IN	TIME OUT	SIGN / INITIAL

Visitor Sign In Sheet

DATE	VISITOR'S NAME	REASON FOR VISIT	TIME IN	TIME OUT	SIGN / INITIAL

Visitor Sign In Sheet

DATE	VISITOR'S NAME	REASON FOR VISIT	TIME IN	TIME OUT	SIGN / INITIAL

Visitor Sign In Sheet

DATE	VISITOR'S NAME	REASON FOR VISIT	TIME IN	TIME OUT	SIGN / INITIAL

Visitor Sign In Sheet

DATE	VISITOR'S NAME	REASON FOR VISIT	TIME IN	TIME OUT	SIGN / INITIAL

Visitor Sign In Sheet

DATE	VISITOR'S NAME	REASON FOR VISIT	TIME IN	TIME OUT	SIGN / INITIAL

Visitor Sign In Sheet

DATE	VISITOR'S NAME	REASON FOR VISIT	TIME IN	TIME OUT	SIGN / INITIAL

Visitor Sign In Sheet

DATE	VISITOR'S NAME	REASON FOR VISIT	TIME IN	TIME OUT	SIGN / INITIAL

Visitor Sign In Sheet

DATE	VISITOR'S NAME	REASON FOR VISIT	TIME IN	TIME OUT	SIGN / INITIAL

Visitor Sign In Sheet

DATE	VISITOR'S NAME	REASON FOR VISIT	TIME IN	TIME OUT	SIGN / INITIAL

Visitor Sign In Sheet

DATE	VISITOR'S NAME	REASON FOR VISIT	TIME IN	TIME OUT	SIGN / INITIAL

Visitor Sign In Sheet

DATE	VISITOR'S NAME	REASON FOR VISIT	TIME IN	TIME OUT	SIGN / INITIAL

Visitor Sign In Sheet

DATE	VISITOR'S NAME	REASON FOR VISIT	TIME IN	TIME OUT	SIGN / INITIAL

Visitor Sign In Sheet

DATE	VISITOR'S NAME	REASON FOR VISIT	TIME IN	TIME OUT	SIGN / INITIAL

Visitor Sign In Sheet

DATE	VISITOR'S NAME	REASON FOR VISIT	TIME IN	TIME OUT	SIGN / INITIAL

Visitor Sign In Sheet

DATE	VISITOR'S NAME	REASON FOR VISIT	TIME IN	TIME OUT	SIGN / INITIAL

Visitor Sign In Sheet

DATE	VISITOR'S NAME	REASON FOR VISIT	TIME IN	TIME OUT	SIGN / INITIAL

Visitor Sign In Sheet

DATE	VISITOR'S NAME	REASON FOR VISIT	TIME IN	TIME OUT	SIGN / INITIAL

Visitor Sign In Sheet

DATE	VISITOR'S NAME	REASON FOR VISIT	TIME IN	TIME OUT	SIGN / INITIAL

Visitor Sign In Sheet

DATE	VISITOR'S NAME	REASON FOR VISIT	TIME IN	TIME OUT	SIGN / INITIAL

Visitor Sign In Sheet

DATE	VISITOR'S NAME	REASON FOR VISIT	TIME IN	TIME OUT	SIGN / INITIAL

Visitor Sign In Sheet

DATE	VISITOR'S NAME	REASON FOR VISIT	TIME IN	TIME OUT	SIGN / INITIAL

Visitor Sign In Sheet

DATE	VISITOR'S NAME	REASON FOR VISIT	TIME IN	TIME OUT	SIGN / INITIAL

Visitor Sign In Sheet

DATE	VISITOR'S NAME	REASON FOR VISIT	TIME IN	TIME OUT	SIGN / INITIAL

Visitor Sign In Sheet

DATE	VISITOR'S NAME	REASON FOR VISIT	TIME IN	TIME OUT	SIGN / INITIAL

Visitor Sign In Sheet

DATE	VISITOR'S NAME	REASON FOR VISIT	TIME IN	TIME OUT	SIGN / INITIAL

Visitor Sign In Sheet

DATE	VISITOR'S NAME	REASON FOR VISIT	TIME IN	TIME OUT	SIGN / INITIAL

Visitor Sign In Sheet

DATE	VISITOR'S NAME	REASON FOR VISIT	TIME IN	TIME OUT	SIGN / INITIAL

Visitor Sign In Sheet

DATE	VISITOR'S NAME	REASON FOR VISIT	TIME IN	TIME OUT	SIGN / INITIAL

Visitor Sign In Sheet

DATE	VISITOR'S NAME	REASON FOR VISIT	TIME IN	TIME OUT	SIGN / INITIAL

Visitor Sign In Sheet

DATE	VISITOR'S NAME	REASON FOR VISIT	TIME IN	TIME OUT	SIGN / INITIAL

Visitor Sign In Sheet

DATE	VISITOR'S NAME	REASON FOR VISIT	TIME IN	TIME OUT	SIGN / INITIAL

Visitor Sign In Sheet

DATE	VISITOR'S NAME	REASON FOR VISIT	TIME IN	TIME OUT	SIGN / INITIAL

Visitor Sign In Sheet

DATE	VISITOR'S NAME	REASON FOR VISIT	TIME IN	TIME OUT	SIGN / INITIAL

Visitor Sign In Sheet

DATE	VISITOR'S NAME	REASON FOR VISIT	TIME IN	TIME OUT	SIGN / INITIAL

Visitor Sign In Sheet

DATE	VISITOR'S NAME	REASON FOR VISIT	TIME IN	TIME OUT	SIGN / INITIAL

Visitor Sign In Sheet

DATE	VISITOR'S NAME	REASON FOR VISIT	TIME IN	TIME OUT	SIGN / INITIAL

Made in the USA
Monee, IL
10 November 2023

46176597R00068